Tanoshii
Ke-Ki

Tanoshii
Ke-Ki

Japanese-Style Baking for All Occasions

Yamashita Masataka

Marshall Cavendish
Cuisine

Editor: Lydia Leong
Designer: Lynn Chin
Photographer: Hongde Photography

Published by Marshall Cavendish Cuisine
An imprint of Marshall Cavendish International

Other Marshall Cavendish Offices:
Marshall Cavendish Corporation. 99 White Plains Road, Tarrytown NY 10591-9001, USA
• Marshall Cavendish International (Thailand) Co Ltd. 253 Asoke, 12th Flr, Sukhumvit 21 Road,
Klongtoey Nua, Wattana, Bangkok 10110, Thailand • Marshall Cavendish (Malaysia) Sdn Bhd,
Times Subang, Lot 46, Subang Hi-Tech Industrial Park, Batu Tiga, 40000 Shah Alam,
Selangor Darul Ehsan, Malaysia

Marshall Cavendish is a trademark of Times Publishing Limited
National Library Board, Singapore Cataloguing-in-Publication Data

Names: Yamashita, Masataka. | Lydia, Leong, editor.
Title: Tanoshii ke-ki : Japanese-style baking for all occasions / author,
Yamashita Masataka ; editor, Lydia Leong.
Description: Singapore : Marshall Cavendish Cuisine, [2016]
Identifiers: OCN 930489682 | ISBN 978-981-46-7793-6 (paperback)
Subjects: LCSH: Cake--Japan | Cooking, Japanese | Cookbooks.
Classification: LCC TX771| DDC 641.86530952--dc23

Printed in Singapore

Dedication

This book is dedicated to my beloved wife Ami
who has worked hand in hand with me in building
this empire of cakes from Japan to Singapore!

Contents

CHIFFON CAKES

Basic Vanilla Chiffon 50

Strawberry Chiffon 52

Yuzu Chiffon 54

Latte Chiffon 56

Walnut & Brown Sugar Chiffon 58

Mixed Spice Chiffon 60

Orange Chiffon with Yoghurt Cream 62

Mochi Kinako Chiffon 64

Charcoal Chiffon 66

Umeshu Chiffon 68

Pumpkin Chiffon 70

Black Sesame Tofu Chiffon 72

Pesto & Tomato Chiffon 74

Curry Chiffon 76

MOUSSE CAKES

Cream Cheese & Lemon Curd Mousse Cake 80

Kinako Mousse Cake 82

Strawberry & Champagne Mousse Cake 84

Sake Tiramisu 86

Raspberry Mousse Cake 88

Honey Carrot Mousse Cake 90

Coconut Chocolate Mousse Cake 92

Coffee Mousse with Vanilla Pudding 94

Passion Fruit Mousse Cake 96

Calpis Mousse Cake 98

Blackcurrant & Yoghurt Mousse Cake 100

Italian Meringue 102

EGG-FREE TREATS

Orange Cake 106

Carrot Juice & Honey Cake 108

Lemon & Tofu Cream Tart 110

Edamame & Sour Cream Crackers 112

WEIGHTS & MEASURES 115

Acknowledgements

I WOULD LIKE TO THANK ALL WHO HAVE MADE THIS BOOK POSSIBLE:

My friend, Lincoln Tan, for helping me with the translation of the recipes and for communicating with the various parties involved.

My editor, Lydia Leong, for working so hard with me to produce this third book, and for continuously rescheduling her activities to accommodate many last minute changes.

The photographer, Liu Hongde, for his tiresome efforts.

The designer, Lynn Chin, for her creative works.
It was great working with this creative team once again.

My brilliant team at Chef Yamashita who helped in so many ways, contributing tremendously to the successful production of this book.

Introduction

Once again, I would like to thank you for your support in purchasing this cookbook. It is only with all the support and encouragement I received for my first two cookbooks, *Tanoshii* and *Tanoshii Wagashi* that I am able to follow up with this third cookbook to share more about baking cakes.

This time, I have decided to also include ingredients that may not be commonly used in making cakes, to offer a fresh taste to the palate, and inspire home bakers to explore using new ingredients in their baking.

Finding the perfect taste and flavour combinations among ingredients has always been a huge challenge not only to cake-lovers who bake for leisure at home, but even to chefs like myself, and I hope the suggestions in this book will be a source of inspiration for your baking adventures.

As it was with the confections included in *Tanoshii* and *Tanoshii Wagashi,* the cakes in this cookbook have also been created to ensure that they are not too cumbersome to be prepared, and that bakers of any skill level would be able to replicate these cakes at home.

Baking cakes should always be an enjoyable affair. Even if the cakes do not turn out as planned, just try again and it will get better the next time around!

Have fun trying out the various recipes in this cookbook, and enjoy your creations with your loved ones!

Yamashita Masataka

Baking Equipment

Baking Tins, Trays and Moulds
A variety of baking tins, trays and moulds are used in this book. Choose those made of stainless steel or aluminium as they wear better and last longer. The type of mould, the size and preparation steps are specificied in the individual recipes.

Bamboo Skewer
A thin skewer is essential for testing if a cake is adequately baked. If a skewer inserted into the centre of the baked cake comes out clean, the cake is done. All ovens are different, so it is extremely important to monitor, observe and test as you bake.

Decorating Turntable
A cake decorating turntable will allow you to decorate cakes in a professional manner, but this is a worthwhile investment only if you intend to decorate cakes frequently.

Digital Kitchen Scale
Precision is of utmost importance in baking and a digital kitchen scale will enable you to measure ingredients with accuracy. Most of the recipes in this book call for weight measurements. Get a scale that can weigh up to 5 kg and has a minimum scale unit of 1 g. The tare function on a digital kitchen scale will allow you to reset the weight of the scale to zero, so you can add ingredients to the same container and weigh them as you go along. Treat your scale well and never store anything on top of it. Ensure that it stays calibrated.

Digital Kitchen Timer
A digital kitchen timer will help ensure baking accuracy. This is necessary only if your oven is not equipped with a timer.

Electric Mixer
Both stand mixers and handheld mixers will work for all recipes in this book, but a stand mixer will lead to more professional results. If you intend to bake seriously and frequently, invest in a good stand mixer with a stainless steel bowl that can handle even the smallest quantity of ingredients.

Measuring Cup
A clear glass measuring cup is recommended for measuring liquid as glass can withstand heat and will not retain grease like plastic. A 500-ml measuring cup is ideal. The liquid measures in this book are weighed, so you can place the measuring cup on your digital kitchen scale when taking liquid measurements.

Measuring Spoons
Measuring spoons are used for measuring small quantities of liquid and powder ingredients precisely. A baker's set should include $1/8$ tsp, $1/4$ tsp, $1/2$ tsp, 1 tsp and 1 Tbsp measures. Both stainless steel and plastic measuring spoons will work well. When measuring out ingredients, be sure to level the contents for accuracy.

Mixing Bowls

Stainless steel mixing bowls are used in professional kitchens as their conductivity means that they can be used effectively in hot or iced water baths. Avoid using plastic bowls as they retain smells and grease. Mixing bowls made of glass are acceptable.

Offset Spatula

Offset spatulas have an angled edge that is useful for removing cookies from baking trays and decorating celebration cakes. A thin metal spatula approximately 23 cm in length will work well for most cakes.

Parchment Paper

Parchment paper is used to line baking tins and trays. It is non-stick and disposable, which makes for easy cleaning. Sifting flour on parchment paper also allows for easy transfer into a mixing bowl. Parchment paper can be folded into a cone and used as a disposable piping bag. Baked goods can also be packaged using parchment paper.

Pastry Brush

A 5-cm wide brush is useful for buttering small cake moulds and ramekins, and applying egg wash. Pastry brushes with natural bristles instead of silicon are preferred. Wash immediately after use and hang to dry to keep your pastry brushes in tip top condition. Replace as soon as the bristles start to shed.

Piping Bags

Piping bags are used to decorate cakes and for piping small amounts of batter. Select bags made of a sturdy material or use disposable ones for ease of cleaning.

Rubber Spatula

A heat resistant rubber spatula is useful for mixing cake batters and folding dry ingredients into the wet. Choose one that is flexible with a good grip and not flimsy.

Scraper

A plastic scraper is preferred for smoothing out the surface of sponge batters because of its lightness and sensitivity, while a stainless steel scraper is preferred for dividing dough.

Serrated Cake Slicer

A long serrated knife is useful for slicing sponge cakes and chiffon cakes without compressing it. A 30–35-cm long serrated cake slicer would suffice for most tasks.

Sieve

A large 16-cm wide sieve with a handle is useful for straining wet ingredients as it can be suspended over a bowl. A similar sieve without a handle is useful for sifting dry ingredients onto parchment paper. A small sieve with a handle is useful for dusting icing sugar or cocoa powder over baked goods. Look for sieves with a sturdy mesh.

Thermometer

A digital instant-read candy thermometer that can read up to 200°C is recommended. Some recipes in this book call for mixtures to reach precise temperatures, so having a candy thermometer is essential when working on those recipes.

Whisk

Choose a stainless-steel whisk with solid and fine wires in a bulbous shape. A whisk with more wires is more efficient. The size of the whisk should correspond to the bowl it is used with. Select a whisk with a nice weight to it, as too light a whisk demands more energy.

Wire Rack

A wire rack or cooling rack allows freshly baked cakes and cookies to cool down efficiently. One that holds your largest baking tin would suffice.

Baking Ingredients

Almond Powder
Almond power, also known as almond flour or almond meal, is made from finely grated blanched almonds. It adds a rich nutty taste to baked goods. Choose finely grated almond powder for the best results.

Baking Powder
Used as a leavening agent in baking. Sift the required amount of baking powder with the other dry ingredients before using to ensure equal distribution.

Butter
Unsalted butter is commonly used for baking because it allows the baker to have more control over the salt content in the baked products. Standard supermarket butter would have 80–81% butterfat content. Keep butter wrapped up in the refrigerator to avoid absorption of refrigerator smells.

Cassis Purée
Made from puréed blackcurrants, cassis purée gives a rich blackcurrant flavour and a lovely purple colour to mousse cakes. It is available from baking supply stores and some gourmet supermarkets.

Charcoal Powder
Charcoal powder was traditionally used for its health benefits, but it is becoming popular as an ingredient in the kitchen. It gives baked products a lovely black colour, which can be otherwise hard to achieve without artificial food colouring.

Chestnut Paste
Chestnuts are a favourite ingredient added to Japanese cakes and desserts especially in the autumn season. Made from fresh cooked chestnuts, chestnut paste is available from baking supply stores and some gourmet supermarkets.

Chocolate
Dark couverture chocolate (58% cocoa) is used in most recipes in this book. Chocolate buttons are preferred in professional kitchens as they are easy to measure, portion and melt down as compared to large slabs of chocolate. Do not store chocolate in the refrigerator because it will absorb moisture and smells. Keep wrapped and store at room temperature.

Cocoa Powder
Cocoa powder is extracted from cocoa beans, leaving behind the fat component which is cocoa butter. In baking, use Dutch-processed (alkalised) unsweetened cocoa powder. Always sift cocoa powder before use.

Cream Cheese

The cream cheese used throughout this book has been specially selected for its creamy and soft texture which is perfect for making soufflé. When using cheese, always use the full-fat option or be ready to compromise on the taste and texture of the final product.

Eggs

All recipes in this book require large eggs that weigh approximately 60 g with shell. The egg white should be about 35 g, and the egg yolk about 20 g. Fresh, free-range eggs are recommended in baking as they help generate more volume when beaten and produce a richer taste. Make a habit of bringing all eggs required in a recipe to room temperature for 30 minutes before using.

Flour

Pastry flour is used in all recipes in this book. It is also known as top flour and is similar to cake flour and Hong Kong flour. These flours have a low protein content which produces light-textured cakes and cookies. Sift all flours before using.

Gelatin

Gelatin comes in sheet form and power form and both need to be bloomed. Sheet gelatin is preferred as it is easier to store, measure, bloom and melt. Powdered gelatin needs to be added together with its blooming liquid, which might alter the overall liquid ratio in the recipe. Sheet gelatin must be bloomed in iced water (especially in Singapore's heat) or parts of it will dissolve into the liquid and you will not get the full amount of gelatin required for the recipe. Keep sheet gelatin wrapped up and store in a cool, dry place.

Honey

Honey is a natural sweetener and, unlike glucose, it adds flavour. Choose an all-natural honey and store in a cool place.

Japanese Plum Liquor

Japanese plum liquor or umeshu is a fruity liquor popular amongst females in Japan. It is lightly sweet and sour, and has an alcohol content of 10–15%. It adds a lovely sweet and sour taste when used as an ingredient in making cakes.

Kinako Powder

This fragrant, nuttty-tasting powder is made from roasted soy beans. It is often used as a coating for *wagashi*, and is increasingly also used to flavour other confections such as cookies and ice cream. In this book, I use it to add a nutty flavour to chiffon cake.

Mascarpone

Mascarpone is a soft Italian cheese usually used in making tiramisu. It goes very well with coffee. Surprisingly, this cheese goes well with sake too.

Milk

Whole milk or full-fat milk is used for all recipes in this book. Avoid low-fat or skim milk, if possible, for the best results.

Mochi Flour

Mochi flour is milled from a Japanese short grain glutinous rice, *mochigome*. It is typically used in making Japanese sweets or *wagashi*, but Japanese chefs have started to use it to create a fusion between Japanese and western cakes. Mochi flour adds a chewy texture to cakes and other treats.

Orange Liqueur

Orange liqueur is used in cocktails, but it is also very popular as a baking ingredient, adding a lovely orange flavour to baked goods. Here, I use it in a mousse cake for its light and refreshing flavour.

Passion Fruit Purée

This brightly coloured fruit purée is available from baking supply stores and some gourmet supermarkets. It is popularly used in cocktails, smoothies and ice cream, and also works well in mousse cakes.

Sakekasu

Sakekasu is a by-product of making Japanese rice wine or sake. It has a high nutritional value and is used in the Japanese kitchen as a marinade or for pickling. I have used it to make a sake tiramisu.

Sugar

Granulated sugar is used in baking not just to provide sweetness but also to stabilise the foaming of eggs and to prevent drying. In baking, use castor sugar, a fine grain sugar, so the grains dissolve more quickly.

Icing sugar, on the other hand, is used mainly for decoration. Icing sugar contains 1–2% cornflour to prevent clumping, but it can still clump up in humid places. Always sift icing sugar if using in batter, and sift it directly onto baked goods if using only for decoration.

Vanilla Extract

Vanilla extract is also often referred to as bourbon vanilla. It is added to impart fragrance to baked goods. Choose a quality extract for the best flavour.

Whipping Cream

Whipping cream is made from milk fat. Try to get cream with more than 35% fat content to produce a silky, light cream when whipped. If required in a recipe here, there is no substitution. Whipping cream cannot be left at room temperature for long periods of time. Store in the refrigerator when not in use.

Yoghurt

In baking, yoghurt is perfect for adding moisture to cakes, but it also helps to dilute the sweetness of other ingredients which would otherwise have been too sweet to be used. It also helps bind flavours together.

Yuzu Honey Tea

Yuzu honey tea is a popular beverage in Japan. Made from thinly sliced yuzu rind and honey, yuzu honey tea is enjoyed for its aromatic, sweet and slightly tangy taste. When used in baking, it adds a light citron flavour to the baked product.

Sponge Cakes & Roll Cakes

Basic Sponge Cake

Makes one 18-cm round sponge

80 g pastry flour
10 g cornflour
15 g unsalted butter
30 g milk
3 eggs
1 egg yolk
10 g glucose
10 g honey
120 g castor sugar

1. Preheat oven to 180°C. Line an 18-cm round baking tin with parchment paper.

2. Sift together pastry flour and cornflour. Set aside.

3. Heat butter and milk in a small saucepan until butter is melted. Remove from heat and set aside.

4. In a medium heatproof bowl, lightly whisk together eggs, egg yolk, glucose, honey and sugar.

5. In a large heatproof bowl, heat some water to 60°C–70°C. Sit medium bowl in large bowl of hot water and whisk until egg mixture is pale and thick. Batter should hold its shape briefly when whisk is lifted. Remove from heat.

6. Sprinkle sifted flour onto mixture from a distance above bowl. Using a rubber spatula, fold in flour. Turn bowl as you fold mixture, scraping base and sides of bowl well.

7. Slowly add melted butter and milk mixture and mix in a circular motion, scraping base and sides of bowl, until just incorporated.

8. Pour batter into prepared tin and bake for 25 minutes until top of cake is golden brown and a skewer inserted into the centre of cake comes out clean.

9. Unmould sponge and place on a wire rack to cool for about 30 minutes before peeling off parchment paper. The sponge is now ready for use.

TIP: Always use clean and dry bowls and tools when mixing cake batters to ensure the baked cake turns out well.

Basic Roll Cake Sponge

Makes one 25-cm roll cake sponge

30 g unsalted butter
35 g milk
4 eggs
1 egg yolk
80 g castor sugar
110 g pastry flour, sifted

1. Line a shallow 25-cm square baking tray with parchment paper. Preheat oven to 200°C.

2. Heat butter and milk in a saucepan until butter is melted. Remove from heat.

3. In a medium heatproof bowl, lightly whisk together eggs, egg yolk and sugar.

4. In a large heatproof bowl, heat some water to 60°C–70°C. Sit medium bowl in large bowl of hot water and whisk until egg mixture is pale and thick. Batter should hold its shape briefly when whisk is lifted. Remove from heat.

5. Sprinkle sifted flour onto mixture from a distance above bowl. Using a rubber spatula, fold in flour. Turn bowl as you fold mixture, scraping base and sides of bowl well.

6. Slowly add melted butter and milk mixture and mix in a circular motion, scraping base and sides of bowl, until just incorporated.

7. Pour batter into prepared tray.

8. Using a plastic scraper, gently smoothen surface of batter in a single direction. Bake for 10–20 minutes or until surface of sponge is golden brown.

9. Test if sponge is done by pressing centre of cake lightly. It should spring back. Place sponge on a wire rack. Peel away parchment paper at the side. Leave to cool for about 30 minutes.

10. Place a cutting board over the sponge and flip it over. Peel off and replace parchment paper at the base and flip sponge back upright. The roll is now ready for use.

Salted Caramel Wrap Cakes

Makes 3 wrap cakes, each 12-cm

1 roll cake sponge,
    25-cm square (page 26),
    chilled

BANANA

1 banana
5 g lemon juice

SALTED CARAMEL SAUCE

200 g whipping cream
20 g water
100 g castor sugar
20 g unsalted butter, melted
1/4 tsp salt

CHANTILLY CREAM

200 g whipping cream
15 g sugar

1. Using a 12-cm round cutter, cut 3 rounds from roll sponge. Cover and set aside.

2. Prepare banana. Peel and cut banana into 5-mm thick rounds and halve them. Drizzle with lemon juice.

3. Prepare salted caramel sauce. Warm cream in a saucepan over low heat. In another pan, heat water and sugar over low heat until sugar is dissolved. Increase to medium heat and stir mixture slowly. When sugar starts to turn brownish, gradually add warmed cream, stirring until mixture is smooth. Add butter and salt and mix well.

4. Prepare Chantilly cream. Using an electric mixer, whisk whipping cream and sugar at high speed until soft peaks form.

5. Mix 200 g Chantilly cream with 40 g salted caramel sauce and whisk until medium soft peaks form.

6. Spoon some salted caramel Chantilly cream onto sponge rounds. Top with banana slices and drizzle with salted caramel sauce. Fold each cake into a semicircle and cover with plastic wrap.

7. Refrigerate cakes for at least 30 minutes before unwrapping to serve. Consume within the day.

TIP: The excess roll sponge can be crumbled and used as sponge crumbs for cake decorating if desired.

Mont Blanc Cakes

Makes three 7-cm round cakes

1 roll cake sponge,
  25-cm square (page 26),
  chilled
4 cooked chestnuts;
  3 whole, 1 chopped
Sponge crumbs, as needed
  (see Tip, page 20)
Icing cugar for dusting

CUSTARD CREAM
3 egg yolks
50 g + 30 g castor sugar
30 g pastry flour, sifted
300 g milk
$1/5$ tsp vanilla extract

CHANTILLY CREAM
200 g whipping cream
15 g castor sugar

MONT BLANC CREAM
450 g whipping cream
300 g chestnut (maron) paste

1. Using a 7-cm round cutter, cut 6 rounds from roll cake. Cover and set aside.

2. Prepare custard cream. In a heatproof mixing bowl, beat egg yolks and 50 g sugar until mixture is pale. Add flour and mix well. Add milk, vanilla extract and 30 g sugar and mix well. Strain into a small pot and stir over medium heat until mixture starts to boil and thicken. Continue stirring until mixture is thick and sticky. Remove from heat. Cover and refrigerate for about 30 minutes.

3. Prepare Chantilly cream. Using an electric mixer, whisk whipping cream and sugar at high speed until soft peaks form.

4. Prepare mont blanc cream. Using an electric mixer, whisk whipping cream at high speed until soft peaks form. Add to chestnut paste and mix well. Whisk until mixture is firm.

5. To assemble cakes, spoon some custard cream over 3 cake layers, then sandwich with remaining cake layers. Cover cakes with Chantilly cream and coat with sponge crumbs if desired. Top each cake with a whole chestnut and pipe Mont Blanc cream over to cover chestnuts. Sprinkle with chopped chestnut and dust with icing sugar. Decorate as desired.

6. Refrigerate for 30 minutes before serving. Consume within the day.

Lychee Shortcake

Makes one 18-cm round cake

1 round sponge, 18-cm wide
  (page 24)
1 can lychees, about 567 g,
  drained and cut into halves

CHANTILLY CREAM
400 g whipping cream
20 g castor sugar

1. Cut sponge horizontally into half. Set aside.

2. Prepare Chantilly cream. Using an electric mixer, whisk whipping cream and sugar at high speed until soft peaks form.

3. Spoon a quarter of Chantilly cream into another bowl and continue to whisk until medium soft peaks form.

4. Spoon half the medium soft cream onto the bottom half of sponge and spread evenly.

5. Arrange lychee halves evenly over medium soft cream and top with remaining medium soft cream. Place top half of sponge over cream and lychee layer.

6. Using a hand whisk, whisk half the remaining Chantilly cream until medium soft peaks form. Spoon on top of cake and spread cream over top and sides of cake.

7. Whisk remaining Chantilly cream until medium soft peaks form. Transfer to a piping bag fitted with a 1-cm star tip. Decorate cake with Chantilly cream and lychee halves.

8. Refrigerate for 30 minutes before serving. Consume within the day.

Rock Melon Layer Cake

Makes one 25 x 12.5-cm cake

1 roll cake sponge,
   25-cm square (page 26),
   chilled

220 g rock melon, cut into
   1-cm cubes + more for
   decorating cake if desired

White chocolate sheet,
   optional

CHANTILLY CREAM

400 g whipping cream

20 g castor sugar

1. Cut roll cake in half to get 2 rectangles. Set aside.

2. Prepare Chantilly cream. Using an electric mixer, whisk whipping cream and sugar at high speed until soft peaks form.

3. Spoon a quarter of Chantilly cream into another bowl and continue to whisk until medium soft peaks form.

4. Spoon half the medium soft cream onto one rectangular sponge and spread evenly.

5. Arrange rock melon evenly over medium soft cream and top with remaining medium soft cream. Place other rectangular sponge over cream and rock melon layer.

6. Whisk half the remaining Chantilly cream until medium soft peaks form. Spread over top of cake.

7. Repeat to whisk remaining Chantilly cream until medium soft peaks form. Transfer to a piping bag fitted with a 1-cm star tip. Decorate cake with Chantilly cream, rock melon and white chocolate if desired.

8. Refrigerate for 30 minutes before serving. Consume within the day.

Mixed Berry Roll

Makes one 25-cm roll cake

1 roll cake sponge,
    25-cm square (page 26)

¾ cup mixed berries
    (blueberries, strawberries
    and raspberries, cut into
    small pieces)

Sponge crumbs, as needed
    (see Tip, page 28)

Icing sugar, for dusting

CHANTILLY CREAM

400 g whipping cream

20 g castor sugar

1. Prepare Chantilly cream. Using an electric mixer, whisk whipping cream and sugar at high speed until medium soft peaks form.

2. Place sponge on a large sheet of parchment paper. Spoon three-quarters of Chantilly cream onto sponge and spread evenly. Top with a layer of mixed berries.

3. Using a long knife, make a line parallel to one side of the cake, 2 cm from the edge. Use this line as the starting point to roll up cake.

4. Roll cake up together with parchment paper, using a long ruler to keep roll straight. Keep cake wrapped up and refrigerate for at least 30 minutes.

5. Transfer remaining Chantilly cream to a piping bag fitted with a decorative piping tip. Trim ends of cake, then decorate with Chantilly cream, sponge crumbs and mixed berries if desired. Dust with icing sugar.

6. Refrigerate for 30 minutes before serving. Consume within the day.

Earl Grey Mascarpone Roll

Makes one 25-cm roll cake

90 g pastry flour, sifted

5 g Earl Grey tea leaves, finely blended

3 eggs

80 g castor sugar

10 g unsalted butter, melted

Fresh fruit, as desired

SYRUP

100 g water

50 g castor sugar

10 g orange-flavoured liqueur

MASCARPONE CREAM

150 g mascarpone

90 g condensed milk

300 g whipping cream

1. Line a shallow 25-cm square baking tray with parchment paper. Preheat oven to 190°C.

2. Mix sifted flour with blended Earl Grey tea leaves.

3. Prepare syrup. Heat water and sugar in a small pan until it reaches 35°C. Remove from heat and stir in liqueur. Set aside.

4. In a mixing bowl, whisk eggs and sugar until mixture is pale. Add flour mixture and mix well with a rubber spatula. Add melted butter and mix well.

5. Pour batter into prepared tray.

6. Using a plastic scraper, gently smoothen surface of batter in a single direction. Bake for 10–20 minutes or until surface of sponge is golden brown.

7. Place sponge on a wire rack. Peel away parchment paper at the side. Leave to cool for about 30 minutes.

8. Place a cutting board over the sponge and flip it over. Peel off and replace parchment paper at the base and flip sponge back upright. Set aside.

9. Prepare mascarpone cream. Using an electric mixer, whisk mascarpone and condensed milk until well mixed. Gradually add whipping cream and whisk until doubled in volume.

10. Brush sponge with syrup, then spoon some mascarpone cream onto sponge and spread evenly.

11. Using a long knife, make a line parallel to one side of the cake, 2 cm from the edge. Use this line as the starting point to roll up cake. Roll cake up together with parchment paper, using a long ruler to keep roll straight.

12. Decorate cake with remaining mascarpone cream and fresh fruit if desired. Refrigerate for at least 30 minutes before serving. Consume within the day.

Yule Log Cake

Makes one 20-cm log cake

50 g pastry flour
12 g cocoa powder
10 g unsalted butter
50 g milk
3 eggs
1 egg yolk
60 g sugar
10 g honey
Roasted almonds, chopped,
   as needed
Icing sugar, for dusting

CHOCOLATE CREAM
30 g chocolate, chopped
30 g whipping cream

CHANTILLY CREAM
400 g whipping cream
30 g castor sugar

1. Line a shallow 25-cm square baking tray with parchment paper. Preheat oven to 190°C.

2. Sift together flour and cocoa powder. Set aside.

3. Heat butter and milk in a saucepan until butter is melted. Remove from heat.

4. In a medium heatproof bowl, lightly whisk together eggs, egg yolk, sugar and honey. In a large heatproof bowl, heat some water to 60°C–70°C. Sit medium bowl in large bowl of hot water and whisk until mixture is pale and thick. Batter should hold its shape briefly when whisk is lifted. Remove from heat.

5. Fold in flour mixture, turning bowl and scraping base and sides of bowl well. Slowly add melted butter mixture and mix, scraping base and sides of bowl, until just incorporated.

6. Pour batter into prepared tin. Using a plastic scraper, gently smoothen surface of batter in a single direction. Bake for 10–20 minutes or until top of sponge is golden brown. Place sponge on a wire rack. Peel away parchment paper at the side. Leave to cool for about 30 minutes.

7. Prepare chocolate cream. Place chocolate in a heatproof bowl set over a pot of simmering water and stir until melted. Remove from heat. Add cream and mix well.

8. Place sponge cake on a large sheet of parchment paper and spread with chocolate cream. Roll up and refrigerate for about an hour.

9. Prepare Chantilly cream. Using an electric mixer, whisk whipping cream and sugar at high speed until medium soft peaks form.

10. Slice one end of cake on the diagonal and place on top of roll cake. Decorate with Chantilly cream and chopped almonds. Dust with icing sugar. Add Christmas ornaments if desired.

Kirsch Torte

Makes one 18-cm round cake

45 g pastry flour
15 g cocoa powder
2 eggs
1 egg yolk
75 g castor sugar
15 g unsalted butter, melted
Sour cherries, for decoration
Milk chocolate shavings,
  for decoration

SYRUP
60 g water
30 g sugar
10 g kirsch

SOUR CHERRY COMPOTE
70 g sour cherry juice
15 g castor sugar
10 g cornflour
170 g sour cherries

CHANTILLY CREAM
150 g whipping cream
10 g castor sugar

1. Line a 18-cm round baking tin with parchment paper. Preheat oven to 190°C.

2. Sift together flour and cocoa powder. Set aside.

3. In a mixing bowl, whisk together eggs, egg yolk and sugar. Using a rubber spatula, mix in flour mixture. Add melted butter and mix until just incorporated.

4. Pour batter into prepared tin and bake for 20–25 minutes until top of cake is golden brown and a skewer inserted into the centre of cake comes out clean. Unmould sponge and place on a wire rack to cool for about 30 minutes before peeling off parchment paper.

5. Prepare syrup. Heat water and sugar in a small pan until it reaches 40°C. Remove from heat and stir in kirsch.

6. Cut sponge cake horizontally in half. Brush cut sides with syrup. Set aside.

7. Prepare sour cherry compote. Boil sour cherry juice and sugar in a small pan over medium heat until sugar is melted. Add cornflour and stir until mixture is thickened. Add sour cherries and cook for another minute. Remove from heat.

8. Prepare Chantilly cream. Using an electric mixer, whisk whipping cream and sugar at high speed until medium soft peaks form.

9. Spoon half the Chantilly cream onto bottom half of sponge and spread evenly. Arrange sour cherry compote evenly over cream and top with half the remaining cream. Place top half of sponge over cream.

10. Transfer remaining cream to a piping bag fitted with a 1-cm round tip. Decorate cake with cream, sour cherries and chocolate shavings if desired.

11. Refrigerate for 30 minutes before serving. Consume within the day.

Banana Chocolate Cake

Makes one 18-cm round cake

48 g pastry flour

5 g cocoa powder

2 eggs

1 egg yolk

50 g castor sugar

25 g unsalted butter, melted

Roasted almonds, chopped,
   for decoration

BANANAS

2 bananas

5 g lemon juice

CHOCOLATE SAUCE

40 g dark chocolate
   (57% cocoa), chopped

80 g + 150 g whipping cream

10 g sugar

CHANTILLY CREAM

400 g whipping cream

30 g castor sugar

1. Line an 18-cm round baking tin with parchment paper. Preheat oven to 190°C. Sift together flour and cocoa powder. Set aside.

2. In a medium heatproof bowl, lightly whisk together eggs, egg yolk and sugar. In a large heatproof bowl, heat some water to 60°C–70°C. Sit medium bowl in large bowl of hot water and whisk until egg mixture is pale and thick. Batter should hold its shape briefly when whisk is lifted. Remove from heat.

3. Fold in flour mixture, turning bowl and scraping base and sides of bowl well. Slowly add melted butter and mix, scraping base and sides of bowl, until just incorporated.

4. Pour batter into prepared tin and bake for 25 minutes until top of cake is golden brown and a skewer inserted into the centre of cake comes out clean. Unmould sponge and place on a wire rack to cool for about 30 minutes before peeling off parchment paper.

5. Prepare bananas. Peel and cut bananas into 5-mm thick rounds. Drizzle with lemon juice.

6. Prepare chocolate sauce. Place chocolate in a heatproof bowl set over a pot of simmering water. Add 80 g cream and mix well. Remove from heat and sit bowl in an ice bath. Stir until mixture hardens slightly. Add 150 g cream and sugar and stir until mixture is smooth. Set aside.

7. Prepare Chantilly cream. Using an electric mixer, whisk whipping cream and sugar at high speed until medium soft peaks form.

8. Cut cake into 3 layers. Spread bottom layer with some Chantilly cream and top with bananas. Repeat layering and top with remaining sponge. Decorate with Chantilly cream, bananas and almonds. Drizzle with chocolate sauce.

9. Refrigerate for 30 minutes before serving. Consume within the day.

Earl Grey & Orange Sponge Cake

Makes one 25-cm round cake

5 g + 10 g Earl Grey tea leaves
80 g pastry flour, sifted
60 g hot water
2 oranges, peeled and cut
   into segments
3 eggs
80 g castor sugar
20 g unsalted butter, melted
Chocolate balls, optional

CHANTILLY CREAM
500 g whipping cream
35 g castor sugar

1. Line a 25-cm round baking tin with parchment paper. Preheat oven to 180°C.

2. Place 5 g Earl Grey tea leaves in a blender and process until fine. Add to sifted flour and mix well. Set aside.

3. Add remaining 10 g Earl Grey tea leaves to hot water and let steep for 2–3 minutes. Strain before using.

4. In a mixing bowl, beat eggs and sugar until mixture is pale. Add flour mixture and mix well with a rubber spatula. Add strained tea and melted butter and mix well.

5. Pour batter into prepared tin and bake for 25 minutes until top of cake is golden brown and a skewer inserted into the centre of cake comes out clean.

6. Unmould sponge and place on a wire rack to cool for about 30 minutes before peeling off parchment paper.

7. Cut sponge cake horizontally in half.

8. Prepare Chantilly cream. Using an electric mixer, whisk whipping cream and sugar at high speed until medium soft peaks form.

9. Spoon half the Chantilly cream onto the bottom half of the sponge and spread evenly. Arrange half the orange segments evenly over cream and top with half the remaining cream. Place top half of sponge over cream.

10. Transfer remaining Chantilly cream to a piping bag fitted with a 1-cm star tip. Decorate cake with cream, remaining orange segments and chocolate balls if desired.

11. Refrigerate for 30 minutes before serving. Consume within the day.

Chiffon Cakes

Basic Vanilla Chiffon

Makes one 17-cm cake

100 g pastry flour
3 g baking powder

EGG YOLK BATTER
4 egg yolks
40 g castor sugar
40 g olive oil
70 g milk
1–2 drops vanilla extract

MERINGUE
5 egg whites
50 g castor sugar

1. Preheat oven to 170°C. Prepare a 17-cm chiffon cake tin.

2. Sift together pastry flour and baking powder. Set aside.

3. Prepare egg yolk batter. In a large bowl, beat egg yolks and sugar until mixture is thick and creamy.

4. Add olive oil gradually while mixing until mixture is smooth.

5. Add milk and vanilla extract and mix well. Set aside.

6. Prepare meringue. Using an electric mixer and a clean, grease-free bowl, whisk egg whites gently until foamy. Gradually add sugar and whisk until firm peaks form.

7. Spoon one-third of meringue into egg yolk batter and mix gently with a rubber spatula.

8. Add flour mixture and mix until incorporated. Add remaining meringue and mix well.

9. Pour batter into chiffon cake tin. Tap tin gently on counter top to release any air bubbles.

10. Bake for 25 minutes, or until a skewer inserted into centre of cake comes out clean. Remove from oven and invert mould on a wire rack. Let cake cool completely before unmoulding.

11. Tap sides of mould to release cake. Slice to serve. Consume within 2 days.

3

4

6

8

Strawberry Chiffon

Makes one 17-cm cake

100 g pastry flour, sifted
3 g baking powder

EGG YOLK BATTER
4 egg yolks
40 g castor sugar
50 g olive oil
50 g milk
100 g strawberry jam

MERINGUE
5 egg whites
50 g castor sugar

1. Preheat oven to 170°C. Prepare a 17-cm chiffon cake tin.

2. Sift together pastry flour and baking powder. Set aside.

3. Prepare egg yolk batter. In a large bowl, beat egg yolks and sugar until mixture is thick and creamy. Add olive oil gradually while mixing until mixture is smooth. Add milk and mix well. Add strawberry jam and mix again. Set aside.

4. Prepare meringue. Using an electric mixer and a clean, grease-free bowl, whisk egg whites gently until foamy. Gradually add sugar and whisk until firm peaks form.

5. Spoon one-third of meringue into egg yolk batter and mix gently with a rubber spatula. Add flour mixture and mix until incorporated. Add remaining meringue and mix well.

6. Pour batter into chiffon cake tin. Tap tin gently on counter top to release any air bubbles.

7. Bake for 30–40 minutes, or until a skewer inserted into centre of cake comes out clean. Remove from oven and invert mould on a wire rack. Let cake cool completely before unmoulding.

8. Tap sides of mould to release cake. Slice to serve. Consume within 2 days.

Yuzu Chiffon

Makes one 17-cm cake

120 g pastry flour
3 g baking powder

EGG YOLK BATTER
4 egg yolks
40 g castor sugar
45 g olive oil
30 g milk
85 g honey yuzu tea syrup

MERINGUE
5 egg whites
50 g castor sugar

CHANTILLY CREAM (OPTIONAL)
400 g whipping cream
20 g castor sugar

1. Preheat oven to 170°C. Prepare a 17-cm chiffon cake tin.

2. Sift together pastry flour and baking powder. Set aside.

3. Prepare egg yolk batter. In a large bowl, beat egg yolks and sugar until mixture is thick and creamy. Add olive oil gradually while mixing until mixture is smooth. Add milk and mix well. Add honey yuzu tea and mix again. Set aside.

4. Prepare meringue. Using an electric mixer and a clean, grease-free bowl, whisk egg whites gently until foamy. Gradually add sugar and whisk until firm peaks form.

5. Spoon one-third of meringue into egg yolk batter and mix gently with a rubber spatula. Add flour mixture and mix until incorporated. Add remaining meringue and mix well.

6. Pour batter into chiffon cake tin. Tap tin gently on counter top to release any air bubbles.

7. Bake for 30–40 minutes, or until a skewer inserted into centre of cake comes out clean. Remove from oven and invert mould on a wire rack. Let cake cool completely before unmoulding.

8. Tap sides of mould to release cake.

9. Prepare Chantilly cream. Using an electric mixer, whisk whipping cream and sugar at high speed until medium soft peaks form.

10. Decorate cake with Chantilly cream, fresh fruit, chocolate balls, dollops of honey yuzu tea syrup and biscuit crumbs if desired.

11. Refrigerate for 30 minutes before serving. Consume within the day.

Latte Chiffon

Makes one 17-cm cake

150 g pastry flour
2 g baking powder
8 g instant coffee powder
10 g hot water
80 g warm milk

EGG YOLK BATTER
4 egg yolks
50 g castor sugar
90 g olive oil

MERINGUE
5 egg whites
70 g castor sugar

1. Preheat oven to 170°C. Prepare a 17-cm chiffon cake tin.

2. Sift together pastry flour and baking powder. Set aside.

3. Mix instant coffee powder with hot water and warm milk. Set aside.

4. Prepare egg yolk batter. In a large bowl, beat egg yolks and sugar until mixture is thick and creamy. Add olive oil gradually while mixing until mixture is smooth. Add coffee-milk mixture and mix well. Set aside.

5. Prepare meringue. Using an electric mixer and a clean, grease-free bowl, whisk egg whites gently until foamy. Gradually add sugar and whisk until firm peaks form.

6. Spoon one-third of meringue into egg yolk batter and mix gently with a rubber spatula. Add flour mixture and mix until incorporated. Add remaining meringue and mix well.

7. Pour batter into chiffon cake tin. Tap tin gently on counter top to release any air bubbles.

8. Bake for 30–40 minutes, or until a skewer inserted into centre of cake comes out clean. Remove from oven and invert mould on a wire rack. Let cake cool completely before unmoulding.

9. Tap sides of mould to release cake. Slice to serve. Consume within 2 days.

Walnut & Brown Sugar Chiffon

Makes one 17-cm cake

110 g pastry flour
3 g baking powder
30 g baked walnuts,
    chopped

EGG YOLK BATTER
3 egg yolks
50 g light brown sugar
40 g olive oil
50 g milk
1–2 drops vanilla extract

MERINGUE
4 egg whites
30 g castor sugar

1. Preheat oven to 170°C. Prepare a 17-cm chiffon cake tin.

2. Sift together pastry flour and baking powder. Set aside.

3. Prepare egg yolk batter. In a large bowl, beat egg yolks and sugar until mixture is thick and creamy. Add olive oil gradually while mixing until mixture is smooth. Add milk and vanilla extract and mix well. Set aside.

4. Prepare meringue. Using an electric mixer and a clean, grease-free bowl, whisk egg whites gently until foamy. Gradually add sugar and whisk until firm peaks form.

5. Spoon one-third of meringue into egg yolk batter and mix gently with a rubber spatula. Add flour mixture and mix until incorporated. Add remaining meringue and mix well.

6. Add walnuts and mix gently.

7. Pour batter into chiffon cake tin. Tap tin gently on counter top to release any air bubbles.

8. Bake for 25 minutes, or until a skewer inserted into centre of cake comes out clean. Remove from oven and invert mould on a wire rack. Let cake cool completely before unmoulding.

9. Tap sides of mould to release cake. Slice to serve. Consume within 2 days.

Mixed Spice Chiffon

Makes one 17-cm cake

80 g pastry flour
3 g baking powder
3 g ground cinnamon
1.5 g ground ginger
2 g dried Italian herb mix

EGG YOLK BATTER
4 egg yolks
45 g castor sugar
70 g olive oil
65 g milk

MERINGUE
5 egg whites
50 g castor sugar

CHANTILLY CREAM (OPTIONAL)
250 g whipping cream
15 g sugar

1. Preheat oven to 170°C. Prepare a 17-cm chiffon cake tin.

2. Sift together flour, baking powder, ground cinnamon and ground ginger. Stir in herb mix. Set aside.

3. Prepare egg yolk batter. In a large bowl, beat egg yolks and sugar until mixture is thick and creamy. Add olive oil gradually while mixing until mixture is smooth. Add milk and mix well. Set aside.

4. Prepare meringue. Using an electric mixer and a clean, grease-free bowl, whisk egg whites gently until foamy. Gradually add sugar and whisk until firm peaks form.

5. Spoon one-third of meringue into egg yolk batter and mix gently with a rubber spatula. Add flour mixture and mix until incorporated. Add remaining meringue and mix well.

6. Pour batter into chiffon cake tin. Tap tin gently on counter top to release any air bubbles.

7. Bake for 25 minutes, or until a skewer inserted into centre of cake comes out clean. Remove from oven and invert mould on a wire rack. Let cake cool completely before unmoulding.

8. Tap sides of mould to release cake.

9. Prepare Chantilly cream. Using an electric mixer, whisk whipping cream and sugar at high speed until soft peaks form.

10. Serve cake with Chantilly cream if desired. Consume within 2 days.

Orange Chiffon with Yoghurt Cream

Makes one 17-cm cake

150 g pastry flour
2 g baking powder

EGG YOLK BATTER
5 egg yolks
60 g castor sugar
75 g olive oil
150 g orange juice
1 orange, grated for zest

MERINGUE
6 egg whites
80 g castor sugar

YOGURT SAUCE (OPTIONAL)
250 g whipping cream
30 g castor sugar
70 g plain yoghurt
10 g orange liqueur
5 g lemon juice

1. Preheat oven to 170°C. Prepare a 17-cm chiffon cake tin.

2. Sift together pastry flour and baking powder. Set aside.

3. Prepare egg yolk batter. In a large bowl, beat egg yolks and sugar until mixture is thick and creamy. Add olive oil gradually while mixing until mixture is smooth. Add orange juice and zest and mix well. Set aside.

4. Prepare meringue. Using an electric mixer and a clean, grease-free bowl, whisk egg whites gently until foamy. Gradually add sugar and whisk until firm peaks form.

5. Spoon one-third of meringue into egg yolk batter and mix gently with a rubber spatula. Add flour mixture and mix until incorporated. Add remaining meringue and mix well.

6. Pour batter into chiffon cake tin. Tap tin gently on counter top to release any air bubbles.

7. Bake for 30–40 minutes, or until a skewer inserted into centre of cake comes out clean. Remove from oven and invert mould on a wire rack. Let cake cool completely before unmoulding.

8. Tap sides of mould to release cake.

9. Prepare yoghurt sauce. Place ingredients for yoghurt sauce in a mixing bowl and beat for about 8 minutes until medium soft peaks form.

10. Decorate cake with yoghurt sauce and fresh fruit if desired.

11. Refrigerate for 30 minutes before serving. Consume within the day.

Mochi Kinako Chiffon

Makes one 17-cm cake

80 g pastry flour
30 g mochi flour
15 g *kinako* (roasted
 soy bean flour)
2 g baking powder

EGG YOLK BATTER
4 egg yolks
30 g castor sugar
40 g olive oil
70 g milk

MERINGUE
5 egg whites
50 g castor sugar

1. Preheat oven to 170°C. Prepare a 17-cm chiffon cake tin.

2. Sift together pastry flour, mochi flour, *kinako* and baking powder. Set aside.

3. Prepare egg yolk batter. In a large bowl, beat egg yolks and sugar until mixture is thick and creamy. Add olive oil gradually while mixing until mixture is smooth. Add milk and mix well. Set aside.

4. Prepare meringue. Using an electric mixer and a clean, grease-free bowl, whisk egg whites gently until foamy. Gradually add sugar and whisk until firm peaks form.

5. Spoon one-third of meringue into egg yolk batter and mix gently with a rubber spatula. Add flour mixture and mix until incorporated. Add remaining meringue and mix well.

6. Pour batter into chiffon cake tin. Tap tin gently on counter top to release any air bubbles.

7. Bake for 30–35 minutes, or until a skewer inserted into centre of cake comes out clean. Remove from oven and invert mould on a wire rack. Let cake cool completely before unmoulding.

8. Tap sides of mould to release cake. Slice to serve. Consume within 2 days.

Charcoal Chiffon

Makes one 17-cm cake

90 g pastry flour
3 g baking powder
10 g charcoal powder

EGG YOLK BATTER
4 egg yolks
30 g castor sugar
40 g olive oil
70 g milk

MERINGUE
5 egg whites
50 g castor sugar

1. Preheat oven to 170°C. Prepare a 17-cm chiffon cake tin.

2. Sift together pastry flour, baking powder and charcoal powder. Set aside.

3. Prepare egg yolk batter. In a large bowl, beat egg yolks and sugar until mixture is thick and creamy. Add olive oil gradually while mixing until mixture is smooth. Add milk and mix well. Set aside.

4. Prepare meringue. Using an electric mixer and a clean, grease-free bowl, whisk egg whites gently until foamy. Gradually add sugar and whisk until firm peaks form.

5. Spoon one-third of meringue into egg yolk batter and mix gently with a rubber spatula. Add flour mixture and mix until incorporated. Add remaining meringue and mix well.

6. Pour batter into chiffon cake tin. Tap tin gently on counter top to release any air bubbles.

7. Bake for 30–40 minutes, or until a skewer inserted into centre of cake comes out clean. Remove from oven and invert mould on a wire rack. Let cake cool completely before unmoulding.

8. Tap sides of mould to release cake. Slice to serve. Consume within 2 days.

Umeshu Chiffon

Makes one 17-cm cake

3 g baking powder
100 g pastry flour, sifted
1 sour plum (from *umeshu*),
    seeded and chopped

EGG YOLK BATTER
4 egg yolks
25 g castor sugar
50 g salad oil
80 g *umeshu* (Japanese
    plum liqueur)

MERINGUE
5 egg whites
50 g castor sugar

1. Preheat oven to 170°C. Prepare a 17-cm chiffon cake tin.

2. Sift together pastry flour and baking powder. Set aside.

3. Prepare egg yolk batter. In a large bowl, beat egg yolks and sugar until mixture is thick and creamy. Add salad oil gradually while mixing until mixture is smooth. Add *umeshu* and mix well. Set aside.

4. Prepare meringue. Using an electric mixer and a clean, grease-free bowl, whisk egg whites gently until foamy. Gradually add sugar and whisk until firm peaks form.

5. Spoon one-third of meringue into egg yolk batter and mix gently with a rubber spatula. Add flour mixture and mix until incorporated. Add remaining meringue and mix well.

6. Add chopped sour plum and mix gently.

7. Pour batter into chiffon cake tin. Tap tin gently on counter top to release any air bubbles.

8. Bake for 30–40 minutes, or until a skewer inserted into centre of cake comes out clean. Remove from oven and invert mould on a wire rack. Let cake cool completely before unmoulding.

9. Tap sides of mould to release cake. Slice to serve. Consume within 2 days.

Pumpkin Chiffon

Makes one 17-cm cake

3 g baking powder
100 g pastry flour, sifted
200 g Japanese pumpkin,
  seeded and rinsed
  (leave green skin on)
50 g milk

EGG YOLK BATTER
4 egg yolks
50 g g castor sugar
50 g olive oil

MERINGUE
5 egg whites
50 g castor sugar

1. Preheat oven to 170°C. Prepare a 17-cm chiffon cake tin.

2. Sift together pastry flour and baking powder. Set aside.

3. Cook pumpkin in the microwave oven on High for 10 minutes or until pumpkin is soft. Cut 80 g pumpkin into small cubes and set aside. Press the remainder through a fine mesh sieve and mix with milk into a purée. Set aside.

4. Prepare egg yolk batter. In a large bowl, beat egg yolks and sugar until mixture is thick and creamy. Add olive oil gradually while mixing until mixture is smooth. Add pumpkin purée and mix well. Set aside.

5. Prepare meringue. Using an electric mixer and a clean, grease-free bowl, whisk egg whites gently until foamy. Gradually add sugar and whisk until firm peaks form.

6. Spoon one-third of meringue into egg yolk batter and mix gently with a rubber spatula. Add flour mixture and mix until incorporated. Add remaining meringue and mix well.

7. Add pumpkin cubes and mix gently.

8. Pour batter into chiffon cake tin. Tap tin gently on counter top to release any air bubbles.

9. Bake for 30–40 minutes, or until a skewer inserted into centre of cake comes out clean. Remove from oven and invert mould on a wire rack. Let cake cool completely before unmoulding.

10. Tap sides of mould to release cake. Slice to serve. Consume within 2 days.

Black Sesame Tofu Chiffon

Makes one 17-cm cake

100 g pastry flour
3 g baking powder
35 g black sesame seeds,
   finely ground

EGG YOLK BATTER

40 g silken tofu, drained
4 egg yolks
30 g castor sugar
40 g olive oil
40 g milk
8 g black sesame paste

MERINGUE

5 egg whites
50 g castor sugar

CHANTILLY CREAM

200 g whipping cream
15 g sugar

1. Preheat oven to 170°C. Prepare a 17-cm chiffon cake tin.

2. Sift together pastry flour and baking powder. Stir in finely ground sesame seeds. Set aside.

3. Prepare egg yolk batter. Push tofu through a fine mesh sieve into a bowl. Add milk and black sesame paste and mix well. Set aside.

4. In a medium bowl, beat egg yolks and sugar until mixture is thick and creamy. Add olive oil gradually while mixing until mixture is smooth. Add tofu mixture and mix well.

5. In a large heatproof bowl, heat some water to 60°C–70°C. Sit medium bowl in large bowl of hot water and stir until mixture is warmed to about 40°C. Remove from heat. Set aside.

6. Prepare meringue. Using an electric mixer and a clean, grease-free bowl, whisk egg whites gently until foamy. Gradually add sugar and whisk until firm peaks form.

7. Spoon one-third of meringue into egg yolk batter and mix gently with a rubber spatula. Add flour mixture and mix until incorporated. Add remaining meringue and mix well.

8. Pour batter into chiffon cake tin. Tap tin gently on counter top to release any air bubbles.

9. Bake for 30–40 minutes, or until a skewer inserted into centre of cake comes out clean. Remove from oven and invert mould on a wire rack. Let cake cool completely before unmoulding.

10. Tap sides of mould to release cake.

11. Prepare Chantilly cream. Using an electric mixer, whisk whipping cream and sugar at high speed until medium soft peaks form. Transfer to a piping bag fitted with a 1-cm round tip. Decorate cake with Chantilly cream and black sesame seeds if desired. If decorated with cream, consume within the day.

Pesto & Tomato Chiffon

Makes one 17-cm cake

100 g pastry flour, sifted
4 g baking powder
2 g dried basil

EGG YOLK BATTER
50 g milk
45 g tomato purée
20 g pesto
4 egg yolks
35 g castor sugar
40 g olive oil

MERINGUE
5 egg whites
50 g castor sugar

1. Preheat oven to 170°C. Prepare a 17-cm chiffon cake tin.

2. Sift together pastry flour and baking powder. Stir in dried basil. Set aside.

3. Prepare egg yolk batter. In a small bowl, combine milk, tomato purée and pesto. Set aside. In a large bowl, beat egg yolks and sugar until mixture is thick and creamy. Add olive oil gradually while mixing until mixture is smooth. Add tomato-pesto mixture and mix well. Set aside.

4. Prepare meringue. Using an electric mixer and a clean, grease-free bowl, whisk egg whites gently until foamy. Gradually add sugar and whisk until firm peaks form.

5. Spoon one-third of meringue into egg yolk batter and mix gently with a rubber spatula. Add flour mixture and mix until incorporated. Add remaining meringue and mix well.

6. Pour batter into chiffon cake tin. Tap tin gently on counter top to release any air bubbles.

7. Bake for 30–40 minutes, or until a skewer inserted into centre of cake comes out clean. Remove from oven and invert mould on a wire rack. Let cake cool completely before unmoulding.

8. Tap sides of mould to release cake. Slice to serve. Consume within 2 days.

Curry Chiffon

Makes one 17-cm cake

100 g pastry flour, sifted
3 g baking powder
30 g curry powder
2 g cayenne pepper

EGG YOLK BATTER
4 egg yolks
40 g castor sugar
45 g olive oil
60 g milk

MERINGUE
5 egg whites
50 g castor sugar

1. Preheat oven to 170°C. Prepare a 17-cm chiffon cake tin.

2. Sift together pastry flour, baking powder, curry powder and cayenne pepper. Set aside.

3. Prepare egg yolk batter. In a large bowl, beat egg yolks and sugar until mixture is thick and creamy. Add olive oil gradually while mixing until mixture is smooth. Add milk and mix well. Set aside.

4. Prepare meringue. Using an electric mixer and a clean, grease-free bowl, whisk egg whites gently until foamy. Gradually add sugar and whisk until firm peaks form.

5. Spoon one-third of meringue into egg yolk batter and mix gently with a rubber spatula. Add flour mixture and mix until incorporated. Add remaining meringue and mix well.

6. Pour batter into chiffon cake tin. Tap tin gently on counter top to release any air bubbles.

7. Bake for 30–40 minutes, or until a skewer inserted into centre of cake comes out clean. Remove from oven and invert mould on a wire rack. Let cake cool completely before unmoulding.

8. Tap sides of mould to release cake. Slice to serve. Consume within 2 days.

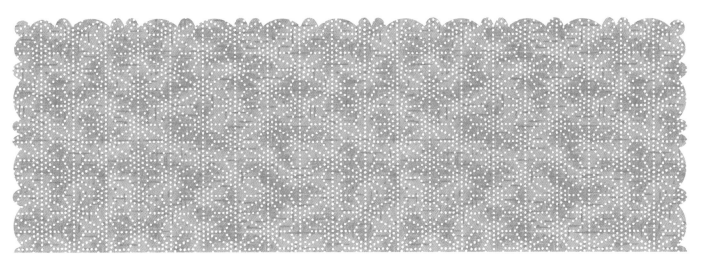

Mousse Cakes

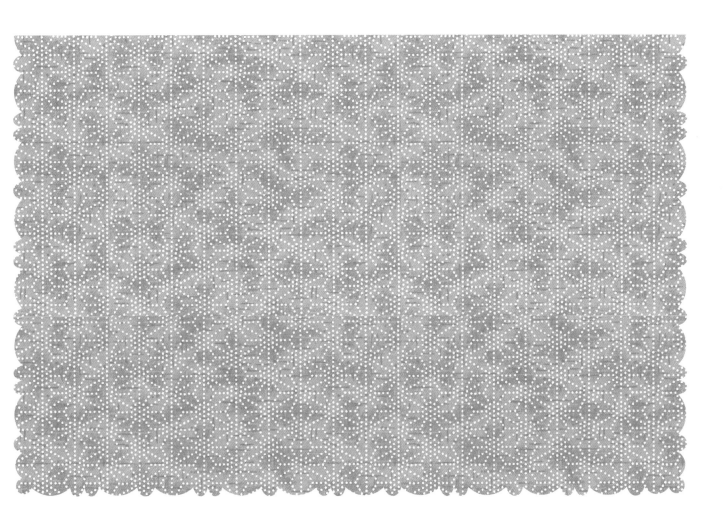

Cream Cheese & Lemon Curd Mousse Cake

Makes 16 oval cakes, each 12-cm long

1 roll cake sponge,
   25-cm square (page 26)

LEMON CURD

Lemon zest, grated from
   1 lemon

Lemon juice, extracted
   from 1 lemon

2 egg yolks

30 g egg whites

60 g castor sugar

30 g unsalted butter

CREAM CHEESE MOUSSE

200 g whipping cream

240 g cream cheese,
   at room temperature

80 g castor sugar

100 g milk

8 g gelatine powder

40 g white wine

CHANTILLY CREAM

200 g whipping cream

15 g sugar

1. Prepare 16 oval silicone moulds, each 12-cm long.

2. Prepare lemon curd. Place all ingredients for lemon curd, except butter, into a heatproof bowl and place bowl over a larger bowl filled with hot water. Whisk until ingredients are well-mixed and sticky. Remove from heat.

3. Add butter and mix well. Pour lemon curd through a strainer into a clean bowl. Cover and set aside.

4. Prepare cream cheese mousse. Using an electric mixer, whisk whipping cream at high speed until soft peaks form. Set aside.

5. In another bowl, whisk cream cheese until softened. Add sugar and whisk until incorporated. Gradually add milk and whisk until mixture is smooth.

6. Sprinkle gelatine over white wine and heat in a microwave oven for about 1 minute on Medium until gelatine is melted. Add to the mixing bowl and mix well.

7. Cut roll cake in half, then cut each half into 8 rectangles.

8. Spoon some cream cheese mousse into each mould until about one-third full. Let set for 10 minutes, then spoon some lemon curd over set mousse. Add another portion of cream cheese mousse, then top with a piece of roll cake. Refrigerate for 1 hour.

9. Prepare Chantilly cream. Using an electric mixer, whisk whipping cream and sugar at high speed until medium soft peaks form.

10. Unmould cakes and decorate with Chantilly cream, fresh fruit and chocolate if desired. Consume within 2 days.

Kinako Mousse Cake

Makes 6 servings

1 roll cake sponge,
   25-cm square (page 26)

KINAKO MOUSSE

7 g gelatine leaf
50 g castor sugar
15 g *kinako* (roasted
   soy bean flour)
200 g warm milk
2 egg yolks
150 g whipping cream

1. Prepare 6 small moulds such as teacups or ramekins.

2. Prepare *kinako* mousse. Place gelatine leaf in a bowl of iced water and set aside to soften.

3. Mix half the sugar with *kinako* powder and mix well. Add a little warm milk and continue to stir until well mixed. Add egg yolks and mix well.

4. Place remaining milk and sugar in a saucepan over medium heat. Add *kinako* mixture and stir until mixture is slightly sticky. Remove pan from heat.

5. Squeeze excess water from gelatin sheet and add to pan. Mix until gelatine is completely dissolved. Strain mixture into a bowl and set aside to cool.

6. Using an electric mixer, whisk whipping cream at high speed until soft peaks form. Add to cooled *kinako* mixture and mix well.

7. Cut roll cake into rounds to fit base of moulds. Pour *kinako* mousse over and refrigerate for about 2 hours or until mousse is set.

8. Decorate with *kinako* and sakura flowers if desired.

Strawberry & Champagne Mousse Cake

Makes 10 small cakes

1 round sponge, 18-cm wide
  (page 24)

STRAWBERRY MOUSSE

3 g gelatine leaf

150 g strawberry sauce

50 g plain yoghurt

80 g whipping cream

CHAMPAGNE MOUSSE

8 g gelatine leaf

150 g egg yolks

160 g castor sugar

330 g champagne

Lemon zest, grated from
  half a lemon

10 g lemon juice

250 g whipping cream

1. Prepare 10 dome-shaped moulds, each about 8-cm wide.

2. Cut sponge cake into 5-mm thick slices, then cut into rounds to fit base of moulds. Cover and set aside.

3. Place gelatine leaves for strawberry mousse and champagne mousse in a bowl of iced water and set aside to soften.

4. Prepare strawberry mousse. Squeeze excess water from 3 g gelatine and place into a bowl with one quarter of strawberry sauce. Mix until gelatine is completely dissolved, then add remaining strawberry sauce and yoghurt.

5. Using an electric mixer, whisk whipping cream at high speed until medium soft peaks form. Add to strawberry mixture and mix well. Refrigerate for about 1 hour.

6. Prepare champagne mousse. Beat egg yolks and sugar until mixture is pale.

7. In another bowl, combine champagne and lemon zest and juice, and heat until 80°C. Squeeze excess water from 8 g gelatine and add to bowl. Mix until gelatine is completely dissolved, then add to egg yolk mixture and mix well. Add whipping cream and mix well. Refrigerate for about 1 hour.

8. To assemble, half fill dome-shaped moulds with champagne mousse, then spoon a little strawberry mousse into the centre of champagne mousse. Divide remaining champagne mousse evenly among moulds, then top with remaining strawberry mousse and seal moulds with a round of sponge cake.

9. Refrigerate for about 2 hours until mousse is fully set.

10. Heat outside of moulds to release cakes. Serve with strawberries and cream if desired. Consume within 2 days.

Sake Tiramisu

Makes 8 servings

1 roll cake sponge,
  25-cm square (page 26)
Cocoa powder for dusting

SAKE SYRUP
60 g castor sugar
15 g honey
90 g water
180 g sake

MASCARPONE CREAM
200 g mascarpone
80 g *sakekasu* (sake lees)
1 whole egg
2 egg yolks
95 g castor sugar
200 g whipping cream

1. Prepare 8 small glasses or ramekins.

2. Cut sponge cake into 5-mm thick slices, then cut into rounds to fit base of moulds. Cover and set aside.

3. Prepare sake syrup. Place sugar, honey and water in a small saucepan. Heat, stirring, until sugar is dissolved. Remove from heat and add sake. Set aside.

4. Prepare mascarpone cream. Mix mascarpone and *sakekasu* in a mixing bowl. Set aside.

5. In a heatproof bowl, whisk egg, egg yolks and sugar, and place over a saucepan of hot water and heat until mixture is foamy. Add to mascarpone mixture and mix well.

6. Brush sponge cake rounds with sake syrup and place into prepared moulds. Add mascarpone cream and refrigerate for 2 hours until set.

7. Dust with cocoa powder before serving. Consume within 2 days.

Raspberry Mousse Cake

Makes 6 small cakes

1 round sponge, 18-cm wide
(page 24)

Chantilly cream (page 80),
if desired

RASPBERRY MOUSSE

3 g gelatine leaves

200 g whipping cream

1 quantity Italian meringue
(page 102)

250 g raspberry purée

1. Prepare 6 small cake rings, each 6-cm wide.

2. Cut sponge cake into 5-mm thick slices. Press cake rings into sliced cake and leave cake in ring as base of mousse cakes. Cover and set aside.

3. Place gelatine leaves in a bowl of iced water and set aside to soften.

4. Using an electric mixer, whisk whipping cream at high speed until soft peaks form. Add to Italian meringue and mix well.

5. Place a quarter of of raspberry purée in a small saucepan and heat gently. Squeeze excess water from gelatine and add to pan. Stir until gelatine is dissolved. Remove from heat and strain into a bowl. Add remaining raspberry purée and mix well.

6. Combine Italian meringue mixture with raspberry purée and mix well.

7. Pour into prepared cake rings and refrigerate for 3 hours or until mousse is set.

8. Spread top of cakes with Chantilly cream before unmoulding if desired.

9. Heat outside of moulds and push to release cakes. Decorate with raspberries and chocolate if desired. Consume within 2 days.

Honey Carrot Mousse Cake

Makes 5 small cakes

5 g gelatine leaf
200 g milk
110 g carrot, peeled
 and sliced
80 g plain yoghurt
40 g castor sugar
50 g honey

1. Prepare 5 small round moulds, each 8-cm wide.

2. Place gelatine leaf in a bowl of iced water and set aside to soften. Squeeze excess water from gelatine, then place in a small saucepan with 50 g milk. Heat gently until gelatine is completely dissolved.

3. Place carrot in a microwave oven and cook for 3–5 minutes on High or until carrot is soft.

4. Place carrot, remaining milk, yoghurt, sugar and honey in a food processor and blend until fine. Pour mixture into a bowl.

5. Add contents of pan to blended carrot mixture and mix well. Strain mixture.

6. Pour mixture equally into prepared moulds and refrigerate for about 2 hours or until mousse is set.

7. Tap mould to release cake. Decorate with Chantilly cream and fresh fruit if desired. Consume within 2 days.

Coconut Chocolate Mousse Cake

Makes 5 small cakes

1 round sponge, 18-cm wide
(page 24)

1 quantity lemon curd
(page 80)

CHOCOLATE LAYER

90 g dark chocolate
(57% cocoa), chopped

70 g whipping cream

10 g unsalted butter,
melted

COCONUT MOUSSE

8 g gelatine leaf

70 g coconut cream
powder

50 g castor sugar

100 g milk

180 g whipping cream

1. Line a 25-cm square baking tray with baking paper. Prepare 5 cake rings, each 6-cm wide. Set aside.

2. Cut sponge cake into 5-mm thick slices. Press cake rings into sliced cake and leave cake in ring as base of mousse cakes. Cover and set aside.

3. Prepare chocolate layer. Place chocolate in a bowl set over a larger bowl filled with hot water. Stir until chocolate is melted.

4. In a small saucepan, bring whipping cream to a simmer. Add to melted chocolate and mix well. Add melted butter and mix again.

5. Pour chocolate mixture into prepared tray. Refrigerate for 3–4 hours until chocolate is set.

6. Prepare coconut mousse. Place gelatine leaf in a bowl of iced water and set aside to soften. Mix coconut cream powder with sugar and set aside.

7. Warm milk in a saucepan. Squeeze excess water from gelatine and add to pan. Stir until gelatine is completely dissolved.

8. Add coconut cream powder mixture to pan and mix well.

9. Using an electric mixer, whisk whipping cream at high speed until medium soft peaks form. Add to pan and mix well. Strain mixture into a bowl.

10. Using a 6-cm cake ring, cut 5 rounds from chocolate layer.

11. To assemble cake, Pour half the coconut mousse equally into prepared cake rings. Top with a chocolate layer and fill mould with remaining coconut mousse. Refrigerate for 3 hours or until mousse is set.

12. Spread lemon curd over set cakes. Heat outside of moulds and push to release cakes. Decorate with fresh fruit and chocolate if desired. Consume within 2 days.

Coffee Mousse with Vanilla Pudding

Makes 4 servings

CARAMEL
80 g castor sugar
50 g water

VANILLA PUDDING
170 g milk
150 g whipping cream
10 g + 10 g castor sugar
¼ vanilla pod
40 g egg yolks
5 g honey

COFFEE MOUSSE
3 g gelatine leaf
100 g whipping cream
30 g castor sugar
8 g instant coffee
50 g milk
15 g hot water

1. Preheat oven to 140°C. Prepare 4 heatproof cups or ramekins, each 8-cm wide and a deep baking tray.

2. Place gelatine leaf for coffee mousse in a bowl of iced water and set aside to soften.

3. Prepare caramel. Heat sugar and water in a small pan over medium heat, stirring until mixture starts to brown and thicken. Pour equally into prepared moulds. Set aside.

4. Prepare vanilla pudding. In a saucepan, heat milk, whipping cream, 10 g sugar and vanilla pod over low heat, stirring until sugar is melted. Set aside to cool.

5. In a bowl, beat egg yolks, honey and 10 g sugar until well mixed. Add milk mixture while stirring and mix well.

6. Strain mixture and pour equally into prepared moulds over caramel. Place moulds into baking tray and fill tray with water until it reaches halfway up the side of moulds.

7. Bake for 35 minutes.

8. Meanwhile, prepare coffee mousse. Using an electric mixer, whisk whipping cream and sugar at high speed until medium soft peaks form. Set aside.

9. In a saucepan, dissolve instant coffee in milk and heat to 40°C. Remove from heat. Squeeze excess water from gelatine and add to pan. Stir until gelatine is completely dissolved. Strain mixture and pour into moulds over baked vanilla pudding.

10. Refrigerate for 2 hours or until mousse is set. Decorate as desired. Consume within 2 days.

Passion Fruit Mousse Cake

Makes 6 servings

CHOCOLATE SPONGE
35 g pastry flour
40 g bread flour
25 g cocoa powder
1 quantity Italian meringue
   (page 102)
90 g egg yolks, beaten

PASSION FRUIT MOUSSE
5 g gelatine leaf
100 g passion fruit purée
75 g egg whites
75 g castor sugar
150 g whipping cream

ORANGE JELLY
4 g gelatine leaf
150 g orange juice
25 g castor sugar

1. Preheat oven to 180°C. Line a 25-cm square baking tray with parchment paper. Prepare 6 ramekins, each 8-cm wide.

2. Sift together pastry flour, bread flour and cocoa powder.

3. Prepare Italian meringue. Add egg yolks and mix well with a rubber spatula. Add sifted flour mixture and mix gently until just incorporated. Pour mixture into prepared baking tray and bake for 20 minutes. Set aside on a wire rack to cool.

4. Using a 6-cm cake ring, cut 6 rounds from chocolate sponge and place into prepared moulds.

5. Prepare passion mousse. Place gelatine leaf in a bowl of iced water and set aside to soften. Gently heat passion fruit purée in a saucepan. Squeeze excess water from gelatine and add to pan. Stir until gelatine is completely dissolved. Strain and set aside.

6. In a mixing bowl, whisk egg whites gently until mixture is foamy. Gradually add sugar and whisk until a firm and glossy meringue is formed. Add passion fruit purée to meringue and mix well.

7. Using an electric mixer, whisk whipping cream at high speed until medium soft peaks form. Add to passion fruit purée and mix well.

8. Pour mousse into prepared moulds over chocolate sponge. Pour any excess mousse into small dome-shaped moulds if desired. Refrigerate for 2 hours until mousse is set.

9. Tap dome-shaped moulds to release mousse and place on top of set mousse in ramekins. Set aside.

10. Prepare orange jelly. Place gelatine leaf in a bowl of iced water and set aside to soften. Gently heat orange juice and sugar in a saucepan. Squeeze excess water from gelatine and add to pan. Stir until gelatine is completely dissolved. Strain and pour over passion fruit mousse. Refrigerate to set.

11. Decorate as desired. Consume within 2 days.

Calpis Mousse Cake

Makes one 20-cm round cake

5 g gelatine leaf
500 g milk
45 g + 10 g lemon juice
75 g Calpis water
400 g whipping cream
40 g egg whites
15 g castor sugar

1. Prepare a 20-cm round cake mould.

2. Place gelatine leaf in a bowl of iced water and set aside to soften.

3. Place milk in a saucepan and heat to 50°C. Remove from heat and stir in 45 g lemon juice. When milk starts to curdle, strain it into a mixing bowl.

4. In a clean saucepan, heat Calpis water and 10 g lemon juice to 50°C. Squeeze excess water from gelatine and add to pan. Stir until gelatine is completely dissolved. Strain and set aside.

5. In a mixing bowl, whisk egg whites gently until mixture is foamy. Gradually add sugar and whisk until a firm and glossy meringue is formed.

6. Fold meringue into Calpis mixture and pour mixture into prepared mould.

7. Refrigerate for 3–4 hours until mousse is set.

8. Unmould cake and and decorate with fresh fruit if desired. Consume within 2 days.

Blackcurrant & Yoghurt Mousse Cake

Makes one 12-cm round cake

1 round sponge, 18-cm wide (page 24)

APPLE CASSIS

10 g castor sugar

20 g cassis (blackcurrant) purée

10 g water

¼ apple, cored, pared and quartered, then cut into 5-mm slices

YOGHURT MOUSSE

5 g gelatine leaf

100 g plain yoghurt

20 g castor sugar

60 g whipping cream

CASSIS MOUSSE

5 g gelatine leaf

65 g cassis (blackcurrant) purée

20 g castor sugar

10 g crème de cassis (blackcurrant liqueur)

70 g whipping cream

1. Prepare a 12-cm cake ring. Cut a 5-mm thick layer from sponge cake and press cake ring into cake. Leave cake in ring as base of mousse cake. Cover and set aside.

2. Start preparations for apple cassis a day ahead. Place sugar, cassis purée and water in a saucepan. Add apple slices and boil until apple softens. Transfer to a bowl and let sit overnight.

3. Place gelatine leaves for yoghurt mousse and cassis mousse in a bowl of iced water and set aside to soften.

4. Prepare yoghurt mousse. Heat yoghurt and sugar in a saucepan until sugar is dissolved. Spoon one-quarter of yoghurt into a bowl. Squeeze excess water from gelatine leaf and add to bowl. Stir until gelatine is completely dissolved. Return mixture to pan and mix well. Using an electric mixer, whisk whipping cream at high speed until medium soft peaks form. Add to pan. Mix well.

5. Strain yoghurt mousse and pour into prepared cake mould. Arrange apple cassis in a layer over yoghurt mousse.

6. Prepare cassis mousse. Heat cassis purée and sugar in a saucepan until sugar is dissolved. Squeeze excess water from gelatine leaf and add to bowl. Stir until gelatine is completely dissolved. Using an electric mixer, whisk whipping cream at high speed until medium soft peaks form. Add to pan. Mix well.

7. Strain cassis mousse and pour into cake mould over apple cassis layer. Refrigerate for 2 hours or until mousse is set.

8. Heat outside of mould to release cake. Decorate with fresh fruit if desired. Consume within 2 days.

Italian Meringue

60 g water
150 g + 40 g castor sugar
120 g egg whites

1. In a saucepan, boil water with 150 g sugar until it reaches 118°C on a candy thermometer.

2. Using a whisk or an electric mixer, whisk egg whites gently until mixture is foamy.

3. Gradually add remaining sugar and whisk until soft peaks form.

4. Gradually add syrup while whisking.

5. Whisk until mixture is smooth and glossy

6. Use as needed.

TIP: If using an electric mixer and the meringue does not seem to be mixing well, reduce the speed of the mixer and continue whisking until the meringue is smooth and glossy.

1

3

4

5

Egg-free Treats

Orange Cake

Makes one 16 x 6.5-cm loaf cake

BATTER

40 g almond powder
60 g mochi flour
35 g brown sugar
1.5 g baking soda
2 g water
30 g olive oil
40 g orange juice

ORANGE SYRUP

30 g brown sugar
100 g water
1 orange, cut half into 5-mm
    slices, the other half diced

1. Preheat oven to 170°C. Line a 16 x 6.5-cm loaf tin with parchment paper.

2. Prepare orange syrup. Place brown sugar and water in a saucepan and heat, stirring, until sugar is dissolved. Remove from heat and add sliced and diced orange. Set aside.

3. Prepare batter. Sift almond powder and mochi flour together into a mixing bowl. Add brown sugar and stir to mix.

4. In a small bowl, mix baking soda with water. Add olive oil and orange juice and mix well.

5. Add to flour mixture with diced orange. Mix with a rubber spatula until ingredients are just incorporated.

6. Pour mixture into prepared loaf tin and level surface. Top with orange slices.

7. Bake for 25 minutes or until a skewer inserted into the centre of cake comes out clean.

8. Unmould cake and leave to cool on a wire rack. Consume within 2 days.

Carrot Juice & Honey Cake

Makes two 16 x 6.5-cm loaf cakes
or one 15-cm round cake

100 g carrot juice
65 g honey
150 g plain flour
2 g baking powder
2 g baking soda
2 g ground cinnamon
1 g allspice
A pinch of salt
60 g brown sugar

1. Preheat oven to 160°C. Line two 16 x 6.5-cm loaf tins or a 15-cm round cake tin with parchment paper.

2. Warm carrot juice in a saucepan. Add honey and stir to dissolve. Set aside.

3. Sift together flour, baking powder, baking soda, ground cinnamon and allspice in a mixing bowl. Add salt and brown sugar and mix well.

4. Add carrot-honey juice and mix with a rubber spatula until ingredients are just incorporated.

5. Pour mixture into prepared cake tin and bake for 50 minutes or until a skewer inserted into the centre of cake comes out clean.

6. Unmould cake and leave to cool on a wire rack. Serve with sour cream if desired. Consume within 2 days.

Lemon & Tofu Cream Tart

Makes one 23-cm round tart

TART BASE
250 g almonds, roasted
35 g plain flour
30 g mochi flour
1 g salt
50 g maple syrup
40 g olive oil

LEMON FILLING
200 g sugar-free soy milk
55 g water
2 g agar agar powder
75 g maple syrup
55 g glucose
1 g salt
Lemon zest, grated
  from 2 lemons
30 g lemon juice
80 g apple juice
25 g cornflour
3 g bread flour

TOFU CREAM
300 g tofu
50 g maple syrup
30 g lemon juice
1 g salt

1. Preheat oven to 180°C. Prepare a 23-cm tart tin.

2. Prepare tart base. Place almonds, plain flour, mochi flour and salt into a food processor and blend until mixture is fine. Transfer to a mixing bowl.

3. Whisk maple syrup and olive oil together. Add to almond mixture and mix well into a dough.

4. Roll dough out on a plastic sheet until it is large enough to line the tart tin. Carefully overturn dough into tart tin and press dough into tin. Trim to neaten edges. Bake for 10–12 minutes.

5. Prepare lemon filling. Place soy milk, water and agar agar powder in a saucepan over medium heat. Bring to the boil, stirring until agar agar is dissolved. Lower heat and add maple syrup, glucose, salt and lemon zest. Simmer for 2 minutes.

6. In a small bowl, mix together lemon juice, apple juice, cornflour and bread flour. Add to pan and stir over low heat until mixture is thick.

7. Pour lemon filling into baked tart shell and let set.

8. Prepare tofu cream. Wrap tofu in a clean tea towel and place between 2 cutting boards. Weigh it down with a bag of flour or sugar and let drain for 30 minutes.

9. Place tofu, maple syrup, lemon juice and salt in a food processor and blend until smooth.

10. Spoon tofu cream over lemon filling and refrigerate for about 1 hour to chill before serving.

11. Decorate with sliced lemons if desired. Consume within 2 days.

Edamame & Sour Cream Crackers

Makes about 40 small crackers

100 g plain flour
1 g baking powder
A pinch of salt
15 g castor sugar
20 g cold butter, cut into
    small cubes
A pinch of black pepper
70 g edamame
20 g sour cream

1. Sift flour and baking powder into a mixing bowl. Add salt and sugar and mix well.

2. Add butter and rub into flour mixture using finger tips until mixture resembles breadcrumbs. Add pepper and mix well.

3. Bring mixture together and wrap with plastic wrap Store refrigerated while preparing edamame.

4. Place edamame in a microwave-safe bowl and cook in a microwave oven on High for about 2 minutes. Remove pods and skin beans. Mash with a fork. Add sour cream and mix well. Set aside.

5. Preheat oven to 170°C. Line a baking tray with parchment paper.

6. Combine flour mixture with edamame mash and knead until dough comes together. Wrap with plastic wrap and refrigerate for 2–3 hours.

7. Lightly dust a work surface with flour and roll dough out into a 2-mm thick sheet. Use a cookie cutter to cut out desired shapes.

8. Arrange on prepared baking tray. Bake for 15 minutes.

9. Place baked crackers on a wire rack to cool.

10. Store cooled crackers in a clean airtight container in a cool place. Crackers will keep for up to 2 weeks.

Weights & Measures

Quantities for this book are given in Metric, Imperial and American (spoon) measures. Standard spoon and cup measurements used are: 1 tsp = 5 ml, 1 Tbsp = 15 ml, 1 cup = 250 ml. All measures are level unless otherwise stated.

LIQUID AND VOLUME MEASURES

Metric	Imperial	American
5 ml	$1/6$ fl oz	1 teaspoon
10 ml	$1/3$ fl oz	1 dessertspoon
15 ml	$1/2$ fl oz	1 tablespoon
60 ml	2 fl oz	$1/4$ cup (4 tablespoons)
85 ml	$2^1/2$ fl oz	$1/3$ cup
90 ml	3 fl oz	$3/8$ cup (6 tablespoons)
125 ml	4 fl oz	$1/2$ cup
180 ml	6 fl oz	$3/4$ cup
250 ml	8 fl oz	1 cup
300 ml	10 fl oz ($1/2$ pint)	$1^1/4$ cups
375 ml	12 fl oz	$1^1/2$ cups
435 ml	14 fl oz	$1^3/4$ cups
500 ml	16 fl oz	2 cups
625 ml	20 fl oz (1 pint)	$2^1/2$ cups
750 ml	24 fl oz ($1^1/5$ pints)	3 cups
1 litre	32 fl oz ($1^3/5$ pints)	4 cups
1.25 litres	40 fl oz (2 pints)	5 cups
1.5 litres	48 fl oz ($2^2/5$ pints)	6 cups
2.5 litres	80 fl oz (4 pints)	10 cups

OVEN TEMPERATURE

	°C	°F	Gas Regulo
Very slow	120	250	1
Slow	150	300	2
Moderately slow	160	325	3
Moderate	180	350	4
Moderately hot	190/200	375/400	5/6
Hot	210/220	410/425	6/7
Very hot	230	450	8
Super hot	250/290	475/550	9/10

DRY MEASURES

Metric	Imperial
30 grams	1 ounce
45 grams	$1^1/2$ ounces
55 grams	2 ounces
70 grams	$2^1/2$ ounces
85 grams	3 ounces
100 grams	$3^1/2$ ounces
110 grams	4 ounces
125 grams	$4^1/2$ ounces
140 grams	5 ounces
280 grams	10 ounces
450 grams	16 ounces (1 pound)
500 grams	1 pound, $1^1/2$ ounces
700 grams	$1^1/2$ pounds
800 grams	$1^1/2$ pounds
1 kilogram	2 pounds, 3 ounces
1.5 kilograms	3 pounds, $4^1/2$ ounces
2 kilograms	4 pounds, 6 ounces

LENGTH

Metric	Imperial
0.5 cm	$1/4$ inch
1 cm	$1/2$ inch
1.5 cm	$3/4$ inch
2.5 cm	1 inch

ABBREVIATION

tsp	teaspoon
Tbsp	tablespoon
g	gram
kg	kilogram
ml	millilitre

I bake because I believe
that a simple but well-made cake
has the potential to bring
joy and laughter to my loved ones.

Chef Yamashita